Bite
into an
Apple

····································

by Lynn Brunelle

BLACKBIRCH®
PRESS

THOMSON
✳
GALE

San Diego • Detroit • New York • San Francisco • Cleveland • New Haven, Conn. • Waterville, Maine • London • Munich

For more information, contact
The Gale Group, Inc.
27500 Drake Rd.
Farmington Hills, MI 48331-3535
Or you can visit our Internet site at http://www.gale.com

LIBRARY OF CONGRESS CATALOGING-IN-PUBLICATION DATA

Brunelle, Lynn
  Bite into an apple / by Lynn Brunelle.
    v. cm. — (Step back science series)
  Includes bibliographical references and index.
  Contents: Where do apples come from? — How do apples get to stores? — How do apples stay fresh in a warehouse? — How do apple growers keep bugs from eating apple trees? — What happens at the end of the apple trees' growing season?
   ISBN 1-56711-675-2 (hardback : alk. paper)
   1. Apples—Juvenile literature. [1. Apples.] I. Title. II. Series.

SB363 .B19 2004
634'.11—dc21   2002153743

Contents   Bite into an Apple

How to Use This Book

Each Step Back Science book traces the path of a science-based act backwards, from its result to its beginning.

Each double-page spread like the ones below explains one step in the process.

Spread 1

Pickers Choose Best Apples

How are the apples at the orchard selected for selling?

The size, color, firmness, and freshness of apples are all factors that help pickers at the orchard choose apples of the highest quality. Their picking, however, is not based solely on opinion. The U.S. Department of Agriculture (USDA) has created standards for grading fruits and vegetables so that the selection process can be consistent and the apples selected in Boise are as fresh as those selected in Boston.

The standard grades are (in order of quality): U.S. Extra Fancy, U.S. Fancy, U.S. #1, and U.S. Utility, though combination grades also exist. These grades all have the same rules of description in terms of color, freedom from disease, cracking, and scabbing. Presence of foreign matter, sunburn, or damage by hail, frost, and drought are other factors.

Pickers at the orchards keep the grades in mind as they select the best apples for each shipment.
But how are apples picked from the trees?

▶ *Apples are sorted and graded according to a rigorous set of standards*

Hands-Off Testing

Apple pickers and USDA inspectors take great pains to learn the art of selecting the highest quality produce. Yet there are some factors that they can still miss—mainly internal defects and contamination that happen underneath an apple's skin.

Because every single apple cannot be tested, USDA inspection tests at a warehouse are done on a random sample of apples brought in by growers. If an apple is even slightly touched by an inspector, it must be discarded. That means, of course, that apples tested by inspectors must always be thrown out.

New technology is being created to test apples without anyone having to handle them. Remote sensing technology—an idea borrowed from the National Aeronautics and Space Administration (NASA)—could allow testing to be done with infrared light away from inspectors' hands. This would allow every single apple to be tested before it reaches consumers.

Bite into an Apple 25

24 STEP BACK SCIENCE

A time line along the top describes all the steps in the process. A marker indicates where each spread is in the process.

A question ends each spread and is repeated as the title of the next spread.

Spread 2

Pickers Take Apples off Trees, Usually by Hand

How are apples picked from the trees?

Most apples are picked by hand and, to minimize bruising, they are carefully placed in bags slung on workers' shoulders. When the bags are full, their contents are gently poured into large wooden bins.

The wooden bins are pulled through the orchard by tractor drivers. When a bin is full, it is placed in cold storage until the apples can be graded and sorted.

Sometimes machines are also used to harvest apples. Machine-picked apples are generally used for cider, juice, applesauce, and vinegar.

Apple harvesting begins in late summer and ends in late autumn. October is National Apple Month because most apples are harvested then.

Aside from the pickers and tractor drivers, there is a support crew that checks the pickers' work. Supervisors make sure that the apples are being picked correctly and that they are sufficiently ripe. A record keeper notes how many apples are picked and how many hours people work.

Whether the apples are picked by hand or machine, bugs are a major concern because just a few could spoil a whole harvest.
So how do apple growers keep bugs from eating apple trees?

▲ *Most apples are picked by hand.*

Ripe for the Picking

As an apple ripens, the cells inside turn starches into sugar and make the apple sweet. If an apple does not have enough time for turning starch into sugar, it is considered immature and will taste sour.

Immature apples can still ripen in time and under the right circumstances. At home, people can ripen an apple by placing it in a paper bag with a banana. The oxygen and other gases such as ethylene that the banana gives off help the apple to mature and begin the process that turns starch into sugar.

Bite into an Apple 27

26 STEP BACK SCIENCE

A short description gives a quick answer to the question asked at the end of the previous step.

Sidebars show interesting related information.

Side Step spreads, like the one below, offer separate but related information.

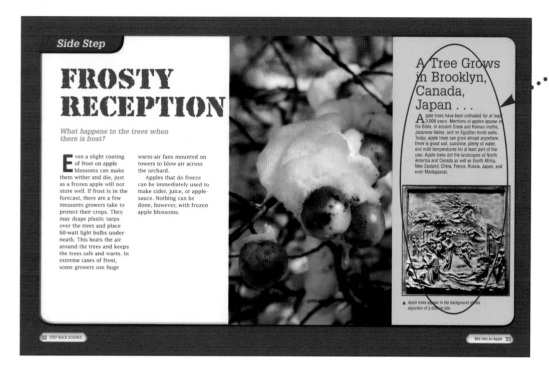

Every Side Step spread contains a sidebar.

The Big Picture, on pages 40–41, shows you the entire process at a glance.

Grocers Stack Apples Carefully to Prevent Bruising

Apples Are Stored in Refrigerated Store Areas

Trucks, Trains, Boats, and Planes Bring Apples to Stores

Apples Picked Up at Refrigerated Warehouse

Wax Coating Added at Warehouse

Bruised Apples Removed for Other Uses at Warehouse

Bite into an Apple

Where do apples come from?

Grab an apple and bite into it. That crunchy, sweet, or sour fruit is a simple, portable, and nutritious snack, but getting it into shoppers' hands takes the efforts of a team of people.

There is a lot of science in apples. Sure, they grow on trees, but there are also machines, chemicals, processes, preservatives, pesticides, and people that help apples keep their crunch as they make their way to grocery store shelves. Every detail counts—even the way apples are displayed. Ask yourself:

Why are apples stacked the way they are?

Apples Packed in Centers Near Orchard

Pickers Choose Best Apples

Pickers Take Apples off Trees, Usually by Hand

Sprayed Chemicals Keep Bugs Away

Growers Thin Apple Trees to Help Apples Grow Properly

Apples Grow in Annual Cycles

Growers Prune Apple Trees to Ready Them for Next Season

New Apple Trees Grow from Grafted Trees

Grocers Stack Apples Carefully to Prevent Bruising

Why are apples stacked the way they are?

Grocery workers pile up the apples, and they give the placement and display of the fruit a lot of thought and care. Since apples have tender skin, or peel, bruising can be a real problem. When an apple bruises, cells burst under its peel. The peel often has tiny breaks, and microorganisms like bacteria can slip inside. An affected spot on the fruit will turn brown and mushy and develop a bitter taste as it rots. Not only that, rotten apples give off gases like carbon dioxide and ethylene. These gases can cause other apples to rot. So one bad apple *can* spoil the whole bunch.

An apple can bruise in several ways. Impact bruising occurs when an apple falls on a hard surface. Compression bruising is a problem when apples are stacked too high and their weight squishes apples in the lower parts of the display. Vibration bruising happens when apples bounce against each other or against their packaging.

Careful piling in a store display is key to apples' condition, as is their location in the store.

Where are the apples kept in the store?

Apples Packed in Centers Near Orchard

Pickers Choose Best Apples

Pickers Take Apples off Trees, Usually by Hand

Sprayed Chemicals Keep Bugs Away

Growers Thin Apple Trees to Help Apples Grow Properly

Apples Grow in Annual Cycles

Growers Prune Apple Trees to Ready Them for Next Season

New Apple Trees Grow from Grafted Trees

▲ Careful stacking helps prevent bruising.

▲ Although fruits can be sold at the same time, each one has its own particular growing season.

The Reason Behind the Season

If the produce section of the grocery store is overflowing with cherries, spring is in the air. When a large variety of gold, red, and green apples decorate the displays, it is probably fall. Though a variety of fruit can be available year-round thanks to international shipping and storage, different fruits have different growing seasons.

Over time, different plants have evolved to ripen at various times of the year. Much of this has to do with the weather and landscape of the parts of the world in which they first evolved.

Apples Are Stored in Refrigerated Store Areas

Where are the apples kept in the store?

Apples must be placed in cool or refrigerated areas of the store with little direct sunlight to live out their full shelf life. Being organic material, apples have a short life span after they stop receiving nourishment from a tree.

As apples ripen, their cells turn starches into sugar. In this process, they take in oxygen and give off carbon dioxide. The process continues even after apples are fully ripe, which eventually causes them to decay. Cooler temperatures slow down the natural processes of the cells. Sugar is created more slowly and waste gas is excreted, or given off, more slowly. In cold temperatures, an apple's ripening processes are almost completely suspended. It does not give off ripening gases and it does not create more sugar. So, to keep fruit from decaying in their displays, grocers put apples in cold storage behind the scenes.

When not part of a display, apples are kept in large walk-in refrigerators in the back of the store.

But how do apples get to stores?

Variety Is the Spice of Life

Apples have been cultivated for thousands of years. In ancient times, Roman farmers experimented with wild apple strains and created approximately twenty different varieties. Today, there are more than two thousand apple varieties. Here are a few of the most popular and the characteristics that make them unique:

Red Delicious: North America's most common snacking apple is sweet with red skin and soft white flesh.

Granny Smith: These are green-skinned, tart, and very crisp, and are best for baking.

Macintosh: These sweet apples have deep red skins and are tapered at the bottom.

Golden Delicious: Mild in flavor and tender-skinned, these are good for baking and making cider.

Winesap: These red-skinned apples are tart and good for cooking.

oxygen

carbon dioxide

▲ As an apple ripens, it takes in oxygen and gives off carbon dioxide.

Bite into an Apple

Grocers Stack Apples Carefully to Prevent Bruising

Apples Are Stored in Refrigerated Store Areas

Apples Picked Up at Refrigerated Warehouse

Wax Coating Added at Warehouse

Bruised Apples Removed for Other Uses at Warehouse

Trucks, Trains, Boats, and Planes Bring Apples to Stores

How do apples get to stores?

Apples travel in shipping containers on refrigerated railroad cars, boats, and planes, and then are trucked to stores. Modern technology provides state-of-the-art refrigeration to keep the apples at a temperature cool enough to let them last as long as possible, yet warm enough to keep them from freezing. An apple that has been frozen is almost as damaged as one that has been bruised. When apples freeze, the liquid in each cell crystallizes and the ice crystals destroy the apple's cells.

Frozen apples that thaw will have a soft, mushy texture.

Before refrigerated shipping techniques were created, apples were transported in cases packed in ice. Inevitably some apples would spoil or freeze, depending on their position near the ice.

Today, refrigerated shipping permits apples to be safely shipped long distances from storage warehouses.

So how do apples stay fresh in a warehouse?

Staying Cool in Cellars

Around 200 years ago, there were no refrigerators, freezers, or handy storage systems like those used today. Instead, people ate only the fruits and vegetables that were in season. Later, they developed ways to preserve fruits and vegetables so they could be eaten during the winter months when few things grew in the earth. Many fruits and vegetables were dried, while others were pickled. Pickling is a process in which salt or vinegar is used to eliminate bacteria so food will not spoil for a long time. Apples, potatoes, beets, carrots, and pears, on the other hand, were stored in underground cellars. The first cellars were simple holes in the ground. Over time these so-called root cellars evolved into underground storage rooms that were very cool and humid. These conditions kept fruits and vegetables cool enough to stay fresh for months.

Shipping containers full of apples (above) stand waiting to travel by trains, boats, or planes, and then to be trucked to stores (below).

Apples Picked Up at Refrigerated Warehouse

How do apples stay fresh in a warehouse?

Before being shipped to stores, apples stay cool in warehouses with huge refrigerated rooms. Computers and technicians constantly monitor these rooms, called controlled atmosphere (CA) storage. CA storage rooms are checked to be sure that they have the right temperature (36°F/2°C) and humidity percentage (95%). Oxygen and carbon dioxide levels are also continually evaluated. Depending on their size, CA storage rooms can hold between ten thousand and one hundred thousand crates of apples at one time.

Storage is not, however, all that happens at the warehouse. The apples' appearances are checked, too.

So what else happens in the warehouse to make apples attractive?

Fairly Fresh Fruit

Nonbruised, crunchy apples seem fresh, but depending on the time of year, they may be up to a year old! Most apples are harvested in August through October and shipped to markets between January and February. Thus, apples in stores between June and July are generally those that have been left for some time in CA storage.

An apple is considered fresh if it is unbruised, firm, and colorful. It must be ripe, with a crisp and crunchy texture. If apples are maintained in a place where temperature, oxygen levels, carbon dioxide, and humidity are controlled, they can stay fresh for up to a year.

Apples Packed in Centers Near Orchard

Pickers Choose Best Apples

Pickers Take Apples off Trees, Usually by Hand

Sprayed Chemicals Keep Bugs Away

Growers Thin Apple Trees to Help Apples Grow Properly

Apples Grow in Annual Cycles

Growers Prune Apple Trees to Ready Them for Next Season

New Apple Trees Grow from Grafted Trees

Top and bottom: Stacks of apple crates in a dome-shaped CA storage building.

Bite into an Apple

Grocers Stack Apples Carefully to Prevent Bruising

Apples Are Stored in Refrigerated Store Areas

Trucks, Trains, Boats, and Planes Bring Apples to Stores

Apples Picked Up at Refrigerated Warehouse

Bruised Apples Removed for Other Uses at Warehouse

Wax Coating Added at Warehouse

What else happens in the warehouse to make apples attractive?

At the warehouse, apples are washed and many are waxed. Apples have a natural coating of wax, called a cuticle, that protects them from losing moisture and keeps them firm. Yet at the warehouse, the apples are washed to remove any dirt or residue that may have accumulated at the apple orchard or during the journey to the warehouse. This washing removes much of the apples' natural wax coating, which is why some warehouse workers give their apples an extra coating of wax.

Fruits and vegetables are about 80 to 90 percent water, so if they did not have a waxy cuticle, they would quickly shrivel. For this reason, people have been waxing fruits and vegetables since the 12th century.

Today, the amount of protective coating is very small. Five tons of apples, which equal approximately thirty thousand apples, are coated with a little more than a gallon (4 liters) of wax. The federal government regulates the process to be sure the wax is safe and the coating kept to a minimum.

Washing and waxing are important, but the first thing that happens to the apples when they get to the warehouse is that they are inspected for bruises and cuts.

So what happens to bruised apples found at the warehouse?

Apples are washed at the warehouse (top). Then a protective coating of wax is applied (right) so they stay juicy.

Organically Grown

▲ *Crops must be grown under strict rules to earn the label "organic."*

When something is labeled "organic," it does not necessarily mean that no chemicals were used in its production. Organic farming can involve the use of selected controlled chemicals refined from natural sources. There are, however, strict guidelines that the U.S. Food and Drug Administration uses to approve foods that come with the organic label. They include:

- Land that is used for organic farming must have had no prohibited substances applied to it for three years.
- Genetically engineered seeds or plants are not allowed.
- Pests, weeds, and bugs must be controlled in a biological, physical, or mechanical method. If that does not work, pesticides from an approved list may be used.

SAUCY STORY

How do some apples get to the store as applesauce?

Many apples are specially selected at the apple orchard to be made into cider, juice, and applesauce because of their sweetness, level of maturity, and color.

Most applesauce is produced in the fall. Apple growers pack apples in large crates and ship them to an applesauce manufacturing plant. There the apples are washed in large tanks of warm water to remove dirt and residue. Cleaned apples then travel along a water pathway or canal to the peeling area. Inspectors take out any apples that are bruised, overripe, or underripe.

Automatic apple-peeling machines core and peel the apples. Peels are saved so they can be squeezed into apple juice, while the apples are passed along to the cooking stage. Before being cooked, they are checked again by inspectors who see that they are all clean, peeled, cored, and fresh.

The apples are placed in a huge pressure cooker that steams and cooks them quickly. When the apples are tender, they are mechanically pushed through a screenlike filter that takes out any remaining seeds, stems, or larger materials and makes the apples into a sauce.

After the sauce cools, it is put into jars that are capped, labeled, packed, and sent out to grocery stores all around the world.

Apples are pushed through a filter (top) as part of a process that results in applesauce (above).

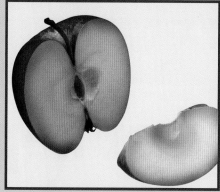

▲ Exposed apple flesh turns brown because of a chemical reaction with the oxygen in the air.

Lemon Fresh

Cut an apple and leave it on a counter for a while and within minutes the apple's white flesh will turn an unappetizing brown. That is because the tissues are exposed to air, which oxidizes them. This reaction is a bit like the way iron oxidizes and rusts when exposed to water.

To prevent browning on a cut or peeled apple, squirt on a little lemon juice. Lemon has a lot of ascorbic acid, or vitamin C. This acid works as a protective coating and prevents the oxygen from affecting the apple. Lemon juice will also prevent browning of potatoes and any other light-colored fruit or vegetable that turns brown when exposed to air.

Bruised Apples Removed for Other Uses at Warehouse

What happens to bruised apples found at the warehouse?

Apples that have bruises and cuts are taken out in the warehouse inspection process and put in separate holding areas. These bruised, broken apples are called seconds or drops because they may have dropped off trees before they could be picked. These apples are used to make cider and juice.

The drops being made into cider are washed, chopped, and loaded into presses, where they are squeezed until all their juice runs out. The dry leftover mash is used for fertilizer or animal food. Fresh cider is filtered to remove any solids, and then bottled, capped, refrigerated, and shipped to stores. Cider is also sometimes flash-pasteurized, which means that it is subjected to very high temperatures for a very brief period of time. This kills micro-organisms but retains the fresh raw flavors. Some cider makers prefer a process that uses ultraviolet light to purify the cider.

To avoid having too many damaged apples in the first place, the fruit must be carefully packed at the orchard where they grow.

So how are the apples at the orchard packed for shipping to the warehouse?

The Raw Deal

Cider or juice? There are real differences.

The biggest difference between cider and apple juice used to be that cider was fresh, raw juice made from squeezed apples and put directly into bottles without being pasteurized. Some roadside stands still sell unpasteurized cider, and some cider lovers claim that is the only "real" cider. But in fact, 98 percent of the cider sold in the United States has been subject to some sort of processing to kill harmful bacteria—either flash-pasteurization or treatment with ultraviolet light.

Another difference is that cider is often made from early-harvest apples, which supposedly have higher acid and lower sugar content, producing a tangy taste. Last, as apple juice is processed, it is filtered and clarified, which changes the look and taste of the juice. Cider does not go through the same amount of filtering. So while apple juice is golden and clear, cider is generally brown and cloudy. Unpasteurized cider often contains a warning label and must be kept refrigerated to keep bacteria at bay.

Damaged apples are squeezed in presses (below left). Their solids are removed (center) and the cider is bottled (right).

Apples Packed in Centers Near Orchard

How are the apples at the orchard packed for shipping to the warehouse?

Large bushels—baskets of approximately one hundred apples—are carefully transported from the orchard to a large nearby packing center. There they are put into cardboard boxes, which are loaded on pallets, or boards. The pallets are put into containing areas on trains, planes, or boats to reach the warehouse.

Of course, the apples are not just dumped into the boxes. Before being packed, apples travel along a water pathway past inspectors who remove any that do not meet quality standards. The flowing waterway helps prevent bruising because it keeps the apples from bumping against each other. To further guard against bruises, packers place paper between layers of apples.

All of this gentle handling of the apples is to ensure they make the journey from the orchards to the consumers in good shape.

But how are the apples at the orchard selected for selling?

▲ *Containers of apples await transport from an orchard to a packing center.*

▲ *Workers pack apples into cardboard boxes at a packing center.*

Use It, Don't Lose It

▲ *Bruised apples may not be bad apples.*

Any fruit that is bumped could be bruised. These bruises, like those on the human body, do not appear right away. They take hours to develop.

There is no need to waste bruised fruit, even at home. Slightly bruised fruit is soft enough to be used in sauces or baked goods. If a fruit is very badly bruised, however, it is best to dump it. The longer fruit decays, the more likely it is that bacteria have taken up residence in it.

Bite into an Apple

Grocers Stack Apples Carefully to Prevent Bruising

Apples Are Stored in Refrigerated Store Areas

Trucks, Trains, Boats, and Planes Bring Apples to Stores

Apples Picked Up at Refrigerated Warehouse

Wax Coating Added at Warehouse

Bruised Apples Removed for Other Uses at Warehouse

Pickers Choose Best Apples

How are the apples at the orchard selected for selling?

The size, color, firmness, and freshness of apples are all factors that help pickers at the orchard choose apples of the highest quality. Their picking, however, is not based solely on opinion. The U.S. Department of Agriculture (USDA) has created standards for grading fruits and vegetables so that the selection process can be consistent and the apples selected in California are as fresh as those selected in Connecticut.

The standard grades are (in order of quality): U.S. Extra Fancy, U.S. Fancy, U.S. #1, and U.S. Utility, though combination grades also exist. These grades all have the same rules of description in terms of color, freedom from disease, cracking, and scabbing. Presence of foreign matter, sunburn, or damage by hail, frost, and drought are other factors.

Pickers at the orchards keep the grades in mind as they select the best apples for each shipment.

But how are apples picked from the trees?

Apples are sorted and ▶ graded according to a rigorous set of standards.

Hands-Off Testing

Apple pickers and USDA inspectors take great pains to learn the art of selecting the highest-quality produce. Yet there are some factors that they can still miss—mainly internal defects and contamination that happen underneath an apple's skin.

Every single apple cannot be tested, so USDA inspection tests at a warehouse are done on a random sample of apples brought in by growers. Apples even slightly touched by an inspector must be discarded because handling may affect results. That means that all apples tested by inspectors must be thrown out.

New technology is being created to test apples without anyone having to handle them. Remote sensing technology—an idea borrowed from the National Aeronautics and Space Administration (NASA)—could allow testing to be done with infrared light, away from inspectors' hands. This would allow every single apple to be tested before it reaches consumers.

Pickers Take Apples off Trees, Usually by Hand

How are apples picked from the trees?

Most apples are picked by hand and, to minimize bruising, they are carefully placed in bags slung on workers' shoulders. When the bags are full, their contents are gently poured into large wooden bins.

The wooden bins are pulled through the orchard by tractor drivers. When a bin is full, it is placed in cold storage until the apples can be graded and sorted.

Sometimes machines are also used to harvest apples. Machine-picked apples are generally used for cider, juice, applesauce, and vinegar.

Apple harvesting begins in late summer and ends in late autumn.

October is National Apple Month because most apples are harvested then.

Aside from the pickers and tractor drivers, there is a support crew that checks the pickers' work. Supervisors make sure that the apples are being picked correctly and that they are sufficiently ripe. A record keeper notes how many apples are picked and how many hours people work.

Whether the apples are picked by hand or machine, bugs are a major concern because just a few could spoil a whole harvest.

So how do apple growers keep bugs from eating apple trees?

| Apples Packed in Centers Near Orchard | Pickers Choose Best Apples | | Sprayed Chemicals Keep Bugs Away | Growers Thin Apple Trees to Help Apples Grow Properly | Apples Grow in Annual Cycles | Growers Prune Apple Trees to Ready Them for Next Season | New Apple Trees Grow from Grafted Trees |

▲ Most apples are picked by hand.

Ripe for the Picking

As an apple ripens, the cells inside turn starches into sugar and make the apple sweet. If an apple does not have enough time to turn starch into sugar, it is considered immature and will taste sour.

Immature apples can still ripen in time and under the right circumstances. At home, people can ripen an apple by placing it in a paper bag with a banana. The oxygen and other gases that the banana gives off, such as ethylene, help the apple to mature and begin the process that turns starch into sugar.

Bite into an Apple

Grocers Stack Apples Carefully to Prevent Bruising

Apples Are Stored in Refrigerated Store Areas

Trucks, Trains, Boats, and Planes Bring Apples to Stores

Apples Picked Up at Refrigerated Warehouse

Wax Coating Added at Warehouse

Bruised Apples Removed for Other Uses at Warehouse

Sprayed Chemicals Keep Bugs Away

How do apple growers keep bugs from eating apple trees?

Most growers of nonorganic apples spray trees with chemicals to keep certain kinds of troublesome bugs away. First, growers learn about the harmful pest's life cycle. Then they use that information to obtain pesticides that kill the insects. Growers spray trees with these pesticides using tractors and airplanes.

Unfortunately for consumers, apples at the grocery store may still have chemical residue on them. That is why it is a good idea to scrub apples with water or store-bought cleansing sprays before eating them.

However, there are federal laws that keep pesticide chemicals and their uses in check. Before a specific chemical mixture can be used, it is tested by federal investigators to be sure the poisons are not dangerous for people or other animals.

Still, some growers choose not to use pesticides. Instead, they bring in certain insects that eat the harmful insects, or they grow plants that naturally repel certain pests.

So how else do apple growers keep trees growing healthily?

| Apples Packed in Centers Near Orchard | Pickers Choose Best Apples | Pickers Take Apples off Trees, Usually by Hand | | Growers Thin Apple Trees to Help Apples Grow Properly | Apples Grow in Annual Cycles | Growers Prune Apple Trees to Ready Them for Next Season | New Apple Trees Grow from Grafted Trees |

▲ *Pesticides are regulated by law and must be tested before use. Some growers choose other ways to control pests.*

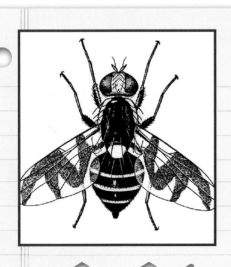

What is an apple maggot?

One major pest to apple growers is the dreaded apple maggot. The tiny adult fly lays her eggs just beneath the skin of an apple. When the eggs hatch, little white maggots that look like tiny rice grains burrow in and begin to eat the flesh of the apple. This spoils it for human consumption.

Growers Thin Apple Trees to Help Apples Grow Properly

How else do apple growers keep trees growing healthily?

One of the essential jobs in growing healthy fruit-producing trees is to cut, or thin, some of their leaves, branches, and fruits as they grow. Once the apples on the trees are the size of Ping-Pong balls, growers snip off small and oddly shaped apples and leave the largest and healthiest of the fruits to mature. Apples that are spaced about 6 inches (15 cm) apart on a branch grow the best.

Growers thin the apple trees for a few different reasons. If every apple were allowed to grow to maturity, the tree would be drained of nourishment and none of the apples would grow large. Furthermore, the tree's health and nutrients would be so taxed that it might not be able to flower the next year. Thinning allows the tree to support fewer fruit so those apples will be large and healthy.

Exposure to sunlight is also important. To begin to ripen and change color, whole apples must be exposed to sunlight. Thinning allows the nourishing rays of light to reach the apple from more angles.

So how do the apples form?

▲ *A tree's smallest apples are removed during the thinning process.*

Apple for the Teacher

Apples have long been valued as a healthful, natural food. They are so cherished, in fact, that they were once used as payment.

The custom of giving a teacher an apple comes from the early days of schooling in the United States, in which public school teachers were given payment directly from parents. When people in small towns and villages did not have enough money, they would pay teachers a small salary and offer a gift of goods, such as chickens, vegetables, and apples. Because apples were small and portable, children would commonly bring them to their teacher at the start of a school day.

FROSTY RECEPTION

What happens to the trees when there is frost?

Even a slight coating of frost on apple blossoms can make them wither and die, just as a frozen apple will not store well. If frost is in the forecast, there are a few measures growers take to protect their crops. They may drape plastic tarps over the trees and place 60-watt lightbulbs underneath. This heats the air around the trees and keeps the trees safe and warm. In extreme cases of frost, some growers use huge warm-air fans mounted on towers to blow air across the orchard.

Apples that do freeze can be immediately used to make cider, juice, or applesauce. Nothing can be done, however, with frozen apple blossoms.

Wintry weather can ▶ devastate an apple crop.

A Tree Grows in Brooklyn, Canada, Japan . . .

Apple trees have been cultivated for at least three thousand years. Mentions of apples appear in the Bible, in ancient Greek and Roman myths, Japanese fables, and on Egyptian tomb walls. Today, apple trees can grow almost anywhere there is good soil, sunshine, plenty of water, and mild temperatures for at least part of the year. Apple trees dot the landscapes of North America and Canada as well as South Africa, New Zealand, China, France, Russia, Japan, and even Madagascar.

▲ Apple trees appear in the background of this depiction of a biblical tale.

Apples Grow in Annual Cycles

How do the apples form?

Apple growth occurs in an annual cycle. In the spring, trees bloom with small blossoms. Inside each blossom are male and female flower parts. The female parts are called the pistils and the male parts are stamens. The stamens produce grains of pollen.

Bees transfer pollen from blossom to blossom and tree to tree to start the process of fruit growth. When pollen reaches the pistils, parts of the grains grow down into the ovary of the flower where fertilization takes place. The blossom reacts by dropping its petals so the fruit can begin to grow. Pollination from different trees assures a better variety of genetic information and better health of the offspring.

All summer long, the leaves on the trees undergo a process to change the sunlight and carbon dioxide that reaches them into sugars, which allows the apple tree to live and grow.

So what happens at the end of the apple trees' growing season?

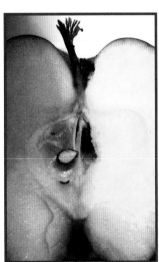

▲ *If you cut an apple open, you can see its parts. The seeds are part of the core, which has formed from the ovaries of the flowers. The dried sepals—parts of the flower that encase the blossom before it blooms—are on the bottom of the apple.*

▲ Growers often bring beehives into their orchard to encourage pollination.

The Buzz on Pollination

In the springtime, apple blossoms bloom, and growers hope for mild weather so bees can do their job of flying from blossom to blossom. This bloom rendezvous is more than just a friendly visit; the bees have an important job to do.

While bees are out gathering nectar for food, they carry pollen on their bodies and bring it from tree to tree and male flower part to female flower part. If there were no bees, there would be no pollination, and no fruit.

Bite into an Apple

Grocers Stack Apples Carefully to Prevent Bruising

Apples Are Stored in Refrigerated Store Areas

Trucks, Trains, Boats, and Planes Bring Apples to Stores

Apples Picked Up at Refrigerated Warehouse

Wax Coating Added at Warehouse

Bruised Apples Removed for Other Uses at Warehouse

Growers Prune Apple Trees to Ready Them for Next Season

What happens at the end of the apple trees' growing season?

To prepare trees to produce fruit each year, apple growers must prune, or shape and cut, the trees between growing seasons. Since trees depend on sunlight to grow and make energy to produce flowers and apples, growers clip and shape the trees so they will have the maximum exposure to sunlight. In a well-shaped tree, the sun shines on every leaf.

Sometimes whole branches are removed until the trees are shaped like upside-down ice-cream cones or Christmas trees. This shape enables sunlight to reach even the trees' lowest branches.

But how are new apple trees made?

▲ *Growers prune their apple trees in winter to prepare them for the approaching spring.*

Apples Packed in Centers Near Orchard

Pickers Choose Best Apples

Pickers Take Apples off Trees, Usually by Hand

Sprayed Chemicals Keep Bugs Away

Growers Thin Apple Trees to Help Apples Grow Properly

Apples Grow in Annual Cycles

New Apple Trees Grow from Grafted Trees

As American as Apple Pie

The expression "as American as apple pie" is quite common. The truth, however, is that apple pie is not necessarily American. The apples used to bake them did not originate in America either.

Apple seeds were first brought to the United States by the British who settled in North America. Yet apples have been around as wild fruit for much longer than that. Ancient Egyptians, Romans, Greeks, and Asians were among the first to grow and snack on apples. An early form of apple pie can be traced back to England, where the tradition of a hot filling inside flaky crust was common.

| Bite into an Apple | Grocers Stack Apples Carefully to Prevent Bruising | Apples Are Stored in Refrigerated Store Areas | Trucks, Trains, Boats, and Planes Bring Apples to Stores | Apples Picked Up at Refrigerated Warehouse | Wax Coating Added at Warehouse | Bruised Apples Removed for Other Uses at Warehouse |

New Apple Trees Grow From Grafted Trees

How are new apple trees made?

For apple growers to produce quality apples every year, they grow new trees from parts of existing healthy trees. In a technique called grafting, growers insert the ends of cut pieces of live trees, called scions, into the base of an adult tree just above the roots. The scions then sprout and, with careful attention from the growers, eventually produce flowers and fruit.

Growers use scions instead of seeds because they want consistent crops.

Waiting to see what quality of tree a seed will produce would be risky and time-consuming for growers.

Different trees may have varied growth habits, nourishment needs, and slight genetic variations that would make the final product different. This is why growers grow trees with the help of a sure ingredient: parts of a healthy, proven tree that produces the exact kind of fruit they hope to sell.

The Legend of Johnny Appleseed

▲ John Chapman founded apple orchards wherever he lived.

A lone man who singlehandedly spread apple seeds around the country, populating America with orchards of apple trees, makes for good storytelling material. The tale of the apple-tree-planting traveler named Johnny Appleseed is based on the actions of a real man. The man who inspired the exaggerated story was John Chapman, an apple lover who was born in Massachusetts in 1774. Around 1797, he traveled west and began to plant apple seeds and seedlings. His interest in apples lasted his whole lifetime. He started several nurseries, grew thousands of trees, had an abundant knowledge of growing apples, and was happy to share this knowledge wherever he went.

Apples Packed in Centers Near Orchard

Pickers Choose Best Apples

Pickers Take Apples off Trees, Usually by Hand

Sprayed Chemicals Keep Bugs Away

Growers Thin Apple Trees to Help Apples Grow Properly

Apples Grow in Annual Cycles

Growers Prune Apple Trees to Ready Them for Next Season

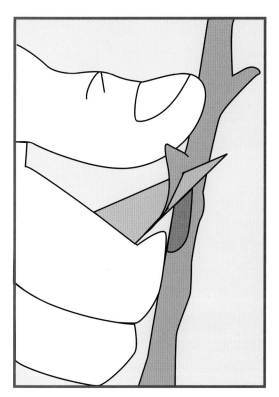
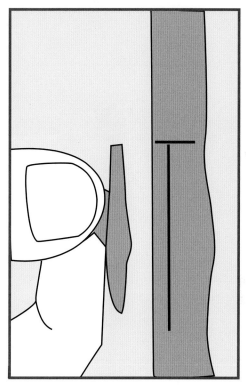
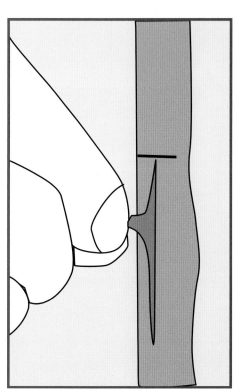
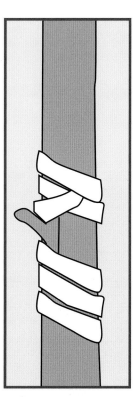
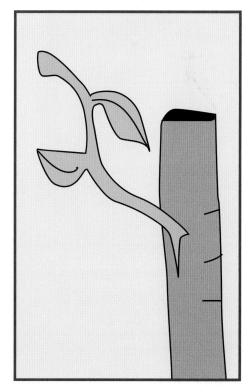

▲ *Grafting uses scions cut from old trees to produce new trees.*

The Big Picture

15 Bite into an Apple

A person bites into an apple.
(pages 6–7)

13 Apples Are Stored in Refrigerated Store Areas

Cool temperatures and no direct sunlight keep apples fresh and prevent them from becoming overripe in stores.
(pages 10–11)

10 Wax Coating Added at Warehouse

Apples are washed and coated with wax to protect them and keep them looking healthy.
(pages 16–17)

14 Grocers Stack Apples Carefully to Prevent Bruising

Grocers stack apples in displays and are careful of damaging the skin of the apple, which can bruise and begin to rot.
(pages 8–9)

12 Trucks, Trains, Boats, and Planes Bring Apples to Stores

Refrigeration technology allows apples to stay cool, but not freeze, while in transit.
(pages 12–13)

11 Apples Picked Up at Refrigerated Warehouse

Controlled atmosphere storage rooms at warehouse keeps apples fresh.
(pages 14–15)

⑨ Bruised Apples Removed for Other Uses at Warehouse

Apples are inspected. Bruised apples may be made into cider.
(pages 20–21)

④ Growers Thin Apple Trees to Help Apples Grow Properly

Less healthy blossoms and apples are thinned out so tree does not waste nourishment on them and sunlight reaches all apples.
(pages 30–31)

③ Apples Grow in Annual Cycles

From pollination to final fruit, apples come from blossoms.
(pages 34–35)

⑧ Apples Packed in Centers Near Orchard

Before apples can be transported, they are packed in cardboard boxes with paper layers between them.
(pages 22–23)

⑤ Sprayed Chemicals Keep Bugs Away

Growers kept pests off plants with pesticides or other insects that will kill the pests.
(pages 28–29)

② Growers Prune Apple Trees to Ready Them for Next Season

Trees are shaped so they receive maximum sun exposure.
(pages 36–37)

⑦ Pickers Choose Best Apples

Workers pick apples based on the fruits' size, color, firmness, and freshness.
(pages 24–25)

⑥ Pickers Take Apples off Trees, Usually by Hand

Apples are harvested by hand or machine by a team of people.
(pages 26–27)

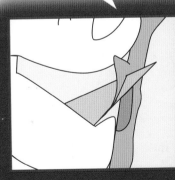

① New Apple Trees Grow from Grafted Trees

New varieties of apples are grafted onto old trunks so healthy trees and apples result.
(pages 38–39)

Core Facts

- It takes an apple tree four or five years to produce its first fruit.
  - The science of growing fruit trees is called pomology.
    - If you cut the top off an apple through the middle, you can see a star shape in the seeds.
  - Apples are about 85 percent water.
  - Apples are a member of the rose family.
- On average, it takes the energy and nutrients created by at least sixty leaves to produce an apple in one season.

VARIETY SHOW

- There are more than two thousand varieties of apples grown in the United States. Apples are grown in every state and in every environment, from desert to forest to grassland, seashore, riverbed, and bog.
- Summer Rambo, Winesap, Rome Beauty, Granny Smith, Strawberry, Kid's Orange Red, Jonagold, Hawaii, and Winter Banana are a few of the apple varieties that exist today.
- Legend has it that Granny Smith apples are named after gray-haired grandma Maria Ann Smith, who first grew them in a suburb of Sydney, Australia.

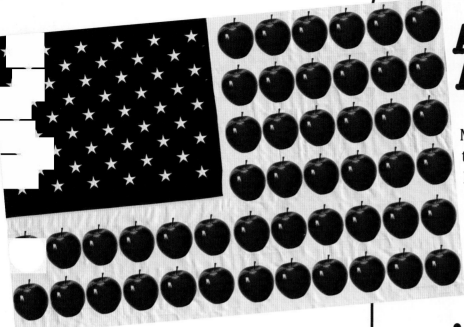

All-American Apples

- The pilgrims of the Massachusetts Bay colony were the first to plant apples in North America. Apple cider was their beverage of choice.
- George Washington and Thomas Jefferson raised apples and exchanged grafting scions with each other in order to grow new varieties.
- John Chapman, also known as Johnny Appleseed, spread apple trees westward.

CAESAR APPLESEED?

Johnny Appleseed was not the first to spread apples by sowing seeds. Ancient Romans planted the apple seeds of about twenty different varieties as they traveled throughout Europe. Now apples grow on every continent except Antarctica.

Wonders and Words

Questions and Answers

Q: *Where are most apples produced?*

A: Although China is the world's largest producer of apples, at least 260 million bushels are grown in the United States each year. More than half of these come from Washington State, but Michigan, New York, California, Pennsylvania, and Virginia are also big apple producers.

Q: *Does an apple a day really keep the doctor away?*

A: No, but apples are a healthful part of a diet. Apples are high in fiber, packed with vitamins, fat-free, sodium-free, and cholesterol-free. Each one has only about 80 calories. Because apples are high in fiber, they help prevent constipation. There are also acids in apples that neutralize the acids in the body and help with indigestion.

Biting into an apple helps prevent gum disease. Apples are somewhat hard, so when they are bitten into, they rub against the gums and allow oxygen inside. This prevents bacterial growth in the gums.

Nutrition Facts

Serving Size   1 medium apple (15g/5.5 oz.)

Amount per Serving

Calories 80   Calories from Fat 0

	% Daily Value*
Total Fat 0g	**0%**
Saturated Fat 0g	**0%**
Cholesterol 0mg	**0%**
Sodium 0mg	**0%**
Potassium 170mg	**5%**
Total Carbohydrates 22g	**7%**
Dietary Fiber 5g	**20%**
Sugars 16g	
Protein 0g	

Vitamin A	2%	Vitamin C	8%
Calcium	0%	Iron	2%

*Percentage Daily Values are based on a 2,000 calorie diet. Your daily values may be higher or lower depending on your calorie needs:

	Calories	2,000	2,500
Total Fat	Less than	60g	65g
Sa Fat	Less than	20g	25g
Cholesterol	Less than	300g	300g
Sodium	Less than	2,400mg	2,400mg
Potassium		3,500mg	3,500mg
Total Carbohydrate		300g	375g
Dietary Fiber		25g	30g

Calories per gram
Fat 9   •   Carbohydrate 4   •   Protein 4

Glossary

Annual: occurring every year

Bushel: baskets of approximately one hundred apples

CA Storage: controlled atmosphere storage

Compression Bruising: bruising that occurs when apples squish against each other

Cultivate: grow

Cuticle: an apple's natural waxy coating

Grafting: the process of joining a living piece of one tree into the trunk of another living tree to produce new growth

Impact Bruising: bruising that occurs when an apple falls on a hard surface

Nectar: the sweet substance of flowers that attracts birds and bees

Nursery: a place where baby trees are grown and cared for

Orchard: a grouping of fruit trees

Ovary: a female part of a flower where fertilization takes place

Pasteurization: the process of treating something with heat to kill harmful bacteria.

Pesticide: a chemical that kills pests

Photosynthesis: the process of creating energy from the sun and carbon dioxide, and water

Pistil: the female part of the flower, where pollen is deposited

Pollination: the process of pollen reaching a pistil

Pruning: trimming and shaping trees to create the best possible growth

Sepal: parts of the flower that encase the blossom before it blooms.

Scion: a living shoot cut from a tree

Stamen: male flower part that produces grains of pollen.

Vibration Bruising: bruising that occurs when apples bump against each other

Index

Credits:

Produced by: J.A. Ball Associates, Inc.
Jacqueline Ball, Justine Ciovacco
Andrew Willett
Daniel H. Franck, Ph.D., Science Consultant

Art Direction, Design, and Production:
designlabnyc
Todd Cooper, Sonia Gauba

Writer: Lynn Brunelle

Cover: Brooke Fasani: boy eating apple; BestApples.com: packing apples, apples being sorted, man picking apple, apple blossom.

Interior: Best Apples.com: p.3 apple blossoms, p.19 applesauce, p.25 apples being sorted, apples in water, p.27 man picking apples, p.35 apple blossom, bees, pp.44–45 apples in water; Brooke Fasani: pp.6–7 boy eating apple, p.8 rotten apples, p.21 girl drinking apple juice, p.23 repulsed girl holding bruised apple; USDA.gov: p.9 apples in grocery store, p.13 boxes in warehouse, p.23 packing center, p.25 USDA inspectors, p.29 truck spraying pesticide, p.30 thinning; Ablestock/Hemera: p.9 multiple fruits, p.10 apples, p.11 apples on tree, p.17 farm, p.19 apple, limes, p.22 boxes of apples, p.31 apple tree, p.32 frosty apples, p.37 bare apple tree, p.37 apple pie, pp.40–41 apple orchard (background); Library of Congress: p.12 cellar images, p.38 Johnny Appleseed; Photospin: p.13: truck, p.14 bitten apple, p.27 grocery bag, p.42 bitten apple, row of apples; Used by permission of the Monolithic Dome Institute: p.15 cold-storage buildings; ColeGraphics.com: p.17 apples being washed and waxed, p.36 pruning; Jonathan and Peggy Morse/The Big Apple: p.19 apples being processed, pp.20–21 apples being made into cider (bottom three photos); ArtToday.com: p.29 apple maggot, p.33 biblical engraving, p.34 center of apple; Sonia "Granny Smith" Gauba: p.39 illustrations of grafting, p.42 apple on branch, p.43 flag with apples, apple map

For More Information

www.appleseed.org
Johnny Appleseed Trail Association in Massachusetts
This site serves as a guide to the Massachusetts area where John Chapman, who became known as Johnny Appleseed, was born. There is information on trails, camping, and recreation in that area, as well as information and links related to the legend of Johnny Appleseed.

www.urbanext.uiuc.edu/apples
The University of Illinois Extension
This site is full of apple facts, fun, and festivals, as well as tips for growing and using apples.

www.usapple.com
U.S. Apple Association
This site gives all kinds of information on apples: health benefits, history, recipes, activities, links to other sites, and a special section for kids.

Otto, Stella. **The Backyard Orchardist: A Complete Guide to Growing Fruit Trees in the Home Garden.** *Maple City, MI: Otto Graphics, 1995.*

Southwick, Larry. **Grafting Fruit Trees.** *Pownal, VT: Storey Books, 1997.*

Warrick, Karen Clemens, **John Chapman: The Legendary Johnny Appleseed (Historical American Biographies).** *Berkeley Heights, NJ: Enslow, 2001.*

Yepsen, Roger. **Apples.** *New York: W.W. Norton, 1994.*